Irina Bagdasaryan

Concretes. Methodological guidelines for the lecture course section "Concretes"

Irina Bagdasaryan

Concretes. Methodological guidelines for the lecture course section "Concretes"

ScienciaScripts

Imprint
Any brand names and product names mentioned in this book are subject to trademark, brand or patent protection and are trademarks or registered trademarks of their respective holders. The use of brand names, product names, common names, trade names, product descriptions etc. even without a particular marking in this work is in no way to be construed to mean that such names may be regarded as unrestricted in respect of trademark and brand protection legislation and could thus be used by anyone.

Cover image: www.ingimage.com

This book is a translation from the original published under ISBN 978-3-659-88666-9.

Publisher:
Sciencia Scripts
is a trademark of
Dodo Books Indian Ocean Ltd. and OmniScriptum S.R.L publishing group

120 High Road, East Finchley, London, N2 9ED, United Kingdom
Str. Armeneasca 28/1, office 1, Chisinau MD-2012, Republic of Moldova, Europe
Managing Directors: Ieva Konstantinova, Victoria Ursu
info@omniscriptum.com

Printed at: see last page
ISBN: 978-620-8-52574-3

Reviewer: Doctor of Technical Sciences, Professor G. G. Shekyan

Author: Candidate of Technical Sciences, Associate Professor Baghdasaryan I.R.

Methodological instructions of the lecture course "Concretes" in the discipline "Construction Materials".

The objectives of lecture classes are outlined, methodical instructions for lectures are given, questions for testing theoretical knowledge are given, basic properties of concrete mixture and concrete, classification, materials for preparation of ordinary (heavy) concrete, peculiarities of concreting in winter time, special types of heavy concrete are outlined.

Methodical instructions are compiled in accordance with the approved program for the subject "Construction materials" for students studying at the specialty 270100 "Construction, building products and production of structures".

CONTENTS

INTRODUCTION

Lecture course of the section "Concretes" is composed of review lectures, using the recommended literature. As a result of studying the section the student should: know the classification of concretes, materials for the preparation of ordinary (heavy) concrete, basic properties of concrete mix and concrete, features of concreting in winter time, special types of heavy concrete.

CHAPTER 1. CONCRETES AND GENERAL CLASSIFICATION OF CONCRETES

1.1 Definition. Classification of concretes.

Objective: to familiarize with concretes, which are classified according to the following main features: by purpose, by average density, by type of binder, by type of aggregates, by structure, by curing conditions.

Concrete (from Fr. *béton) is an* artificial masonry building material obtained by molding and hardening of a rationally selected and compacted mixture consisting of a binder (cement or other), coarse and fine aggregates, and water. In some cases, it may have special additives in its composition, as well as not containing water (e.g., asphalt concrete). Concrete has been known for more than 4000 years (Ancient Mesopotamia), especially widely used in ancient Rome. Italy is a volcanic country where components from which concrete can be made are readily available, including pozzolans and lava rubble. The Romans used concrete in the mass construction of public buildings and structures, including the Pantheon, whose dome is still the largest in the world made of unreinforced concrete. At the same time in the eastern part of the state this technology did not spread, there in construction traditionally used stone, and then cheap plintha - a kind of brick. Due to the decline of the Western Roman Empire, the large-scale construction of monumental buildings and structures came to naught, which made the use of concrete impractical and, combined with the general degradation of craftsmanship and science, led to the loss of its production technology. In the early Middle Ages, the only major architectural objects were cathedrals, which were built of stone.

Modern concrete on cement binder has been known since 1844 (I. Johnson). A patent for Portland cement was obtained in 1824 by Joseph Aspdin; a patent for "Roman cement" was obtained in 1796 by James Parker.

Concrete is one of the basic building materials, without which no construction site can do without. *Foundations, slabs, lintels* and many other structures are made on its basis. They are valued for their strength and durability. But the production of different structures will require the use of different types of concrete. For example, different situations will require *different strength,* level of resistance to moisture and other indicators. This is why the production of different types of concrete is practiced today.

1.1. CONCRETE CLASSIFICATION

Concrete is an artificial masonry material obtained by the hardening of a properly selected, thoroughly mixed and compacted mixture of binder, water, aggregates and, where necessary, special additives. The mixture of the above components before it begins to harden is called a *concrete mixture.* Cement batter, formed after mixing the concrete mixture with water, envelopes grains of sand and gravel, fills the gaps between them and plays the role of lubrication of aggregates, giving the concrete mixture mobility (fluidity). Cement batter, when hardening, binds the grains of aggregates, forming an *artificial stone.*

Nowadays, concrete is the most important building material, produced according to a specific technology depending on the conditions of use. Additional ingredients in the concrete composition improve its technical and structural parameters.

Concretes are classified according to the following main features: by purpose, by average density, by type of binder, by type of aggregates, by structure and by curing conditions.

The following concretes are distinguished ***by purpose***: ordinary and special types of concrete: hydraulic, concrete for transportation construction, road, heat-resistant, structural - thermal insulation, corrosion - resistant, etc.

Depending on the purpose, the following types of concrete mixes are distinguished:

- ordinary concrete is used to create foundations, beams, slabs, columns;
- certain types of concrete are used for the construction of sidewalks, airfields and road surfaces;
- hydrotechnical concrete is used for the construction of canals, sluices, dams, waterworks;
- Special purpose concrete can be acid resistant, heat resistant, radiation protection.

Hydrotechnical concrete includes concrete used for the construction of hydraulic structures (dams, water-regulating, water intake and other structures).

Concretes for transportation construction are designed for the construction of bridges, overpasses, overpasses, culverts and regulation structures on railways and roads.

Road concrete is concrete used in road surfaces, airfields and other similar structures.

The working conditions of road concrete are unfavorable. It is repeatedly subjected to moistening and drying, freezing and thawing, as well as to the impact of vehicles. The main design stresses are bending stresses. In this regard, road concrete is subject to higher requirements for flexural tensile strength, frost resistance, wear resistance and air resistance. The durability of road concrete is achieved not only by the choice of quality materials, but also by the correct technology of work. Portland cement of high grades with organic content of C_3A, high-strength quality aggregates - crushed stone from granite, limestone, quartz sand, etc. are used for road concrete. To increase the mobility of the concrete mixture, plasticizing and air-involving additives are used, and sometimes curing gas pedals.

Structural - heat-insulating concretes are designed for reinforced concrete structures, which are subject to requirements both in terms of load-bearing capacity and heat-insulating properties.

Corrosion-resistant concrete is concrete capable of resisting the action of aggressive media under operating conditions.

Depending on the average density, a distinction is made between extra heavy, heavy, lightweight, lightweight, lightweight and extra lightweight (insulating) concrete. The density of concrete directly affects such characteristics as compressive strength, frost resistance and water resistance. Density is affected by large aggregates concrete mix - expanded clay, gravel, diabase, dolomite, limestone, granite. Concrete density grades from M50 to M800.

Specially heavy concrete with an average density of 2500 kg/m³ is made on especially heavy aggregates (magnetite, barite, iron shot, steel scraps). They are used for special constructions, for example, in the construction of buildings of nuclear power plants for protection against radioactive radiation, and also used in the construction of special facilities with the possibility of resisting radioactive contamination.

Heavy concrete with an average density of 1800 - 2500kg/m³ is made on dense sand and coarse aggregate from dense rocks and used in all load-bearing structures. Heavy concrete is produced when using rocks - granite, diabase, limestone. The density of heavy concrete is 1800-2500 kg/m^3. According to GOST marking of heavy concrete varies from M50 to M800. Field of application: concrete and reinforced concrete structures in civil and industrial buildings and structures, including hydraulic engineering and transportation facilities.

Lightweight lightweight with average density up to 1800 kg/m³ are made on porous coarse aggregate and used for load-bearing structures.

Lightweight concrete with an average density of 500 - 1800kg/m³ is made on porous coarse aggregate and porous or dense fine aggregate. They are mainly used for the production of enclosing or load-bearing structures.

Particularly lightweight concrete (cellular) with an average density of less than 500kg/m³ is made on the basis of a binder and a pore-forming agent. They are used as thermal insulation material in the form of slabs.

According to the type of binder, concretes are divided into: cement, lime binder, gypsum, slag-alkali, etc. The type of binder is the main factor determining the properties of the concrete mixture.

Concretes with lime *binders* are made with lime, quartz sand, slag, ash, active mineral additives. Concretes on lime and silica component, which harden during autoclave treatment, are called silicate concretes. The most widespread are silicate concretes on quartz sand. They are used in industry and civil construction for the manufacture of wall blocks, panels, facing slabs; cellular concretes are also used for thermal insulation.

Cement concrete and *cement mortar* are based on cement components. The most widely used components here are all varieties of Portland cement, Portland slag cement, pozzolanic cement. Also used concrete produced on the basis of shrinkage-free, tensile and alumina cement. Here we can also highlight and decorative concrete, made on the basis of white and colored cements. The color palette of concrete mixes includes blue, red, yellow, black, brown, green and white (the most expensive) colors.

Slag-alkali concrete is a relatively recent development. This type of concrete is created on the basis of slag mixed with alkali solutions. Places of use - erection of large objects. During the construction of massive structures with the use of concrete mixture based on Portland cement is the release of a large amount of heat energy, which contributes to the heating of building elements up to 80 ° C, and with rapid cooling in the concrete structure is a high probability of cracks. The use of slag-alkali concrete helps to avoid this negative effect.

Acid-resistant and heat-resistant concrete contains liquid glass, glass - alkaline and slag elements as binders. It is used in the erection of special construction projects.

Polymer cement concrete results from the use of a mixed binder base that contains latexes, water-soluble resins and cement. When the concrete mixture cools, a film appears on the surface, which tends to swell in the presence of significant amounts of moisture. Polymer-cement concrete is used in landscaping, interior and exterior finishing work, and flooring. With this type of concrete can be worked both manually and mechanized. A distinction is made between framed and filled polymer-cement concrete.

Combined types of concrete include a base of several binding elements. It is used in plaster mixtures containing gypsum, cement, lime and other components.

Gypsum concrete, produced on the basis of gypsum, finds its application in the manufacture of suspended ceilings, interior partitions and in finishing elements. In the construction of bathrooms, gypsum-cement-puzzolana mixtures with high water resistance are used.

Silicate concrete is very rarely used nowadays. The production of silicate concrete is associated with the use of lime and autoclave curing method. This type of concrete can be used in slab panels, in bearing panels of large blocks and internal walls, in tubing for mine construction, and in road foundations. Particularly strong types of silicate concrete are used in railway sleepers, as well as in the production of asbestos-free slate.

According to the type of aggregates used in concrete, they come in dense, porous and special aggregates.

Concrete on dense aggregates is made on aggregates from rocks or industrial waste with an average density of more than 2000kg/m^3. For example, granite crushed stone, metallurgical slag.

Concretes on porous aggregates are made on aggregates with average density less than 2000kg/m^3. For example, expanded clay gravel and sand, agloporite crushed stone and sand, etc. or obtained from porous rocks - tuffs, limestone, etc.

Concretes on special aggregates are made on aggregates obtained from materials that give concrete certain properties. For example, aggregates from iron ores of limonite, hematite, having increased density, absorb radioactive rays.

According to the coarseness of grains of aggregates distinguished fine-grained and coarse-grained: *fine-grained concrete* is *concrete* in which the grain size of coarse aggregate is not larger than 10mm; *in coarse-grained concrete grain* size of coarse aggregate more than 10mm, with a maximum grain size of 40mm.

Depending on the nature of the structure, the following types of concrete are distinguished: *concrete of dense (fused) structure,* in which the space between the grains of aggregates is densely occupied by hardened binder. The permissible volume of inter-grain voids in the compacted concrete mixture does not exceed 6%; *large-porous concretes (sandless or low-sand),* in which a significant part of the volume of inter-grain voids remains unoccupied by fine aggregate and hardened binder; *porous concretes*, in which the space between aggregate grains is occupied by binder, porous foam or gas-forming additives. *Cellular* concrete - concrete with artificially created cells - pores, consisting of a mixture of binder, finely dispersed silica component and pore-forming additive.

According to the type of *coarse porous aggregate* the following types of lightweight concrete are established: keramsite concrete, shungizite concrete, agloporite concrete, slag-pumice concrete, perlite concrete, concrete on crushed stone from porous rocks, vermiculite concrete, slag concrete (concrete on fuel or porous waste metallurgical slag), concrete on agloporite or ash gravel.

The strength of concrete is determined by its grade. Differences in the strength of concrete grades depend on the proportions of cement, sand and crushed stone in its composition. High strength of concrete is obtained by the significant presence of cement.

The strength of concrete indicates its mechanical properties and resistance to loads. It is measured in kgf/cm^2. Concrete of grades M15-M50 is used for the construction of enclosing and heat-insulating structures. For the erection of simple structures (for example, for the bridge of the foundation) is used concrete with low grades: M50-M100. M100-M150 concrete is used for monolithic foundations. For reinforced concrete panels and blocks, which do not experience a serious load, concrete M200 - M250 is used, and for pre-stressed structures concrete mortar with a mark not lower than M300 is used. Concrete M200 is used for construction of railroad slabs and in the process of floor screeding. Concrete with mark M550 is considered to be the most durable. Concrete is categorized by compressive strength classes from B1 to B22. Both systems are designed to take into account the same thing. But there is one difference: the concrete class (B) indicates the guaranteed value, while the concrete grade (M) indicates the average compressive strength value. The guaranteed density value means that the concrete has a strength of at least the stated strength. Although it is more common to classify concrete by grade (M), the guaranteed strength value (B) is specified in the design documents.

1.2. MATERIALS FOR NORMAL (HEAVY) CONCRETE

Portland cement. Stronger concretes are produced with cements of higher activity. Portland cement grades 200, 300, 400 are used for concrete preparation. Numbers mean compressive strength in kg/cm2). Portland cement is a grayish-green fine ground powder. To obtain concrete of different properties and purposes are used varieties of Portland cement: white (or colored on the basis of white), fast hardening, hydrophobic, building; sulfate-resistant, plasticized, pozzolanic and slag Portland cement. Setting of cement, as a rule, comes not earlier than 45 minutes, and ends not later than 24 hours after mixing with water. Full hardening and strength gain usually takes place within 28 days.

The type of cement should be selected in accordance with the purpose of the structures and their operating conditions, the required class (grades) of concrete, the value of the concrete strength for precast structures. Cement consumption in concrete will be rational if the ratio between cement grades and concrete strength is observed (see Table 1). The activity of cement decreases when it is stored in warehouses. Thus, it decreases by 20% after 3 months and 40% after 6 months. Quick-setting cements become ordinary cements after two weeks. To eliminate this phenomenon, the mixing time of the concrete mixture should be increased two to four times and cement hardening gas pedal additives should be used.

Table 1 Relationship between cement grade and strength.

Concrete grade	M100	M150	M200	M300	M400	M500	M600
Concrete class	B 7.5	B10	B15	B25	B30	B40	B50
Cement grade	300	300	400	400	500	550-600	600

When this ratio decreases, cement consumption increases, shrinkage deformations develop, and the crack resistance of concrete decreases; when this ratio increases due to insufficient cement content, concrete mixture delamination is observed, and concrete density decreases.

Sand, which can be natural or artificial, is used *as fine aggregate* in heavy concrete.

Natural sand is a loose mixture of grains with grain size from 0.14 to 5 mm, obtained as a result of natural destruction (weathering) of rocky rocks.

Artificial sand is obtained by crushing hard rocks or some industrial by-products such as metallurgical slags. The shape of the grains of crushed sands is sharp and the surface is rough. These sands do not contain harmful impurities that are often found in natural sands. Sand for concrete should be composed of grains of different sizes so that its inter-grain voids are minimized; the smaller the volume of voids in the sand, the less cement is required to produce dense concrete. The determination of the grain composition of sand is given in the practicals section. Depending on the grain composition, sand is distinguished as coarse, coarse, medium, fine and very fine (Table 2). To ensure the quality of the grain composition of sand in the composition of the concrete mix used fractionated sand, composed of two fractions: coarse and fine, separately dosed in the preparation of concrete mix. Use as fine aggregates crushed sands from the sands and their mixtures with natural sands is allowed provided that the specified workability of the concrete mixture without overconsumption of cement. Bulk density of silica sand depends on the degree of compaction, moisture content and hollowness. Dry and loosely packed quartz sand has a bulk density of 1500 - 1600kg/m^3. The lowest bulk density of quartz sand corresponds to a moisture content of 5 - 7%. When batching sand for concrete production or acceptance of sand, it is necessary to take into account its water content. To determine the grain composition of sand use a standard set of sieves with holes (mm): 10; 5; 1,25; 0,63; 0,315 and 0,14, through which sifted a weight of sand, equal to 1 kg. First determine the private residues in percent on each sieve (a2.5; a1.25; a0.63, etc.), and then the total residues (A2.5; A 1.25; A0.63, etc.). The total residue on any sieve is equal to the sum of the partial residues on that sieve and on all the sieves above it. For example, A0.63 = a0.63 + a0.125 + a2.5. And the values of total residues are a characteristic of the grain composition of sand. Based on the results of sieve analysis of sand, the grain size modulus M_{kr} can be calculated using the formula:

$$M_{(kr)} = (A2.5 + A1.25 + A0.63 + A0.315 + A0.14) / 100$$

Table 2

Grain composition of sand

Sand group	Total residue on the sieve with 0.63mm aperture size, % by weight	Coarse modulus, m_{kr}
coarse	over 65 to 75	More than 3.0 to 3.5
Large	over 45 to 65	More than 2.5 to 3.0
Medium	over 30 to 50	More than 2.0 to 2.5
Shallow	more than 10 to 30	More than 1.5 to 2.0
Very small	up to 10	More than 1.0 to 1.5

Gravel or crushed stone is used *as coarse aggregate* for making heavy concrete.

Crushed stone differs from gravel by its sharp-angled shape and roughness of grains, which makes its adhesion to cement-sand mortar better than that of gravel. *Crushed* stone is obtained by crushing massive rocks, gravel, boulders or artificial stones.

Slag crushed *stone* is produced by crushing slag, which is formed in the process of blast furnace smelting of metals (blast furnace slag) or during combustion of mineral fuel (fuel slag). Slags must have a crystalline structure and show no signs of decay. Slag decomposition is the result of transition of some slag compounds into others under the action of gases contained in the air and moisture. By physical and mechanical properties slag crushed stone should meet the same requirements as natural stone crushed stone. *Frost resistance of gravel and crushed stone* is determined by alternate freezing and thawing in a saturated state of water, as well as accelerated method - freezing in a solution of sodium sulfate. According to the degree of frost resistance gravel and crushed stone are divided into grades: F15, 25, 50, 100, 150, 200 and 300.

Fillers are stored on specially designated open areas or in warehouses equipped with trestles, underground galleries, in stacks separately by types and fractions. In the process of transportation, unloading and storage it is necessary to make sure that there is no mixing of aggregates of different types, as well as their contamination with foreign impurities. In winter time it is necessary to provide measures for loosening of frozen aggregates, as well as for their thawing and heating.

In concrete technology, water is used to prepare concrete mixtures and mortar, to water concrete during curing, and to wash aggregates. In all cases, not any water can be used, but only water that meets the technical specifications. Water quality is assessed by the content of harmful impurities that may prevent normal setting and hardening of the binder or cause the appearance of new formations in the structure of concrete, reducing the strength and durability of concrete. Thus, for mixing concrete and watering the hardening concrete can be used without prior inspection drinking water, as well as river, lake or water from artificial reservoirs, not contaminated with sewage, salts and oils. With the development of concrete production technology, various kinds of additives that improve the properties of concrete mixture and improve the quality of concrete are becoming more and more widespread.

Concrete admixtures. With the development of concrete production technology, various kinds of additives that improve the properties of the concrete mixture and increase the quality of concrete are becoming more and more common.

Plasticizing admixtures are additives that increase the mobility (or reduce the stiffness) of concrete mixtures without reducing the strength of the concrete. Plasticizing additives are surface active substances. According to the nature of action distinguish hydrophilic-plasticizing and hydrophobic-plasticizing additives. Among the hydrophilic-plasticizing additives the most frequently used is LOT (former name SDB). According to its chemical composition it is a calcium salt of lignosulfonic acid with admixture of mineral substances. It is usually supplied in liquid form with a dry matter content of about 50% or in solid form with 80% dry matter content. For plasticization of concrete mixture and mortar it is introduced in a small amount: 0.1-0.5% of the weight of cement. Consumption of the additive: 0.5-1 kg/m^3 of concrete mixture.

Hydrophobic plasticizing additives include soaponaft (sodium salt of naphthenic acids), asidolmylonaft, hydrophobizing organosilicon liquids GKZh-10 and GKZh-11. It is recommended to use these additives in lean concrete and mortars characterized by low cement consumption. After placing and hardening of concrete such additives, precipitating in the pores, give the concrete water-repellent properties (hydrophobize concrete). As a result, the water absorption of concrete is greatly reduced, and at the same time the frost resistance and corrosion resistance of concrete increases. The use of such additives is an effective way to increase the durability of concrete and reinforced concrete structures.

Additives regulating the setting of concrete mixtures and curing of concrete: accelerating or slowing down the setting, accelerating curing, antifreezing.

In practice, the following concrete hardening gas pedals are more often used: calcium chloride (CC), sodium sulfate (SN), calcium nitrate (CN) and sodium nitrate (SN), as well as multi-component additives: calcium nitrite-nitrate (CNN), calcium nitrite-nitrate-chloride (CNNC).

Among the setting retarders, it is best to use additives that reduce both water and cement consumption, as well as plasticizing concrete mixtures and mortar. In this regard, good results are given by organic substances (LST) and organosilicon liquids GKZh-10 and GKZh-11. In addition, use the addition of double-water gypsum, a weak solution of sulfuric acid. The concentration of additives varies from 0.2 to 2% and is established in the laboratory.

Anti-freeze additives are used to ensure that concrete hardens in winter. At sub-zero temperatures, water freezes and cement hydration stops. The resulting ice loosens the still weak structure of the cement stone, causing a large loss of strength in the concrete. To ensure the hardening of concrete in the cold, introduce into the concrete mixture substances that lower the freezing point of water. Water remains in the liquid state even at -15 ... -20 ° C, and the process of cement hydration continues. The following salts are used as anti-freeze additives: sodium chloride in combination with calcium chloride, sodium nitrite, complex compound of calcium nitrate with urea.

Additives reducing cement consumption are mineral powders, industrial by-products: pulverized ash from thermal power plants, blast furnace and fuel slags in fine ground form.

Methodological instructions for the lecture. It is necessary to determine on what signs are classified concretes, to note the difference of concretes on the coarse aggregate on the average density, to know the requirements for sand, water, as well as to pay attention to the existing conditions of hardening concrete.

Questions to test theoretical knowledge.

1. By what characteristics are concretes classified?
2. What concretes are distinguished by average density?
3. Which mineral inorganic binders can be used to prepare concrete mixes?

4. What aggregates are used to make concrete?

5. What are the requirements for coarse aggregate?

6. What are the requirements for sand used for concrete preparation?

7. What groups are sand divided into by grain size?

8. What kind of water is used for concrete mix preparation? Requirements for water for concrete.

9. What are additives that increase the mobility (or decrease the stiffness) of concrete mixtures without decreasing the strength of the concrete called?

10. What anti-freeze additives are used?

11. What are some concrete curing gas pedals?

CHAPTER 2. BASIC PROPERTIES OF CONCRETE MIXTURE AND CONCRETE

Objective: to study the basic properties of ordinary (heavy) concrete, which characterize the quality of hardened concrete.

Hardened concrete is of the composite (conglomerate) type, as it includes obviously heterogeneous components - aggregate grains bound together by cement stone. Therefore, the most important properties that determine the quality of cement stone are strength and adhesion, i.e. the ability to bond with aggregate grains.

Plasticity and mobility of concrete mix. Formability of concrete mixture is determined by two indicators - plasticity and mobility. *Plasticity* characterizes the internal cohesion of the concrete mixture, its ability to be formed, acquiring a given shape without breaks and delamination into separate components.

The *mobility of the concrete mixture* is assessed by its ability to spread under its own weight or under vibration. To determine the mobility is used a cone (Fig. 1), which is filled with concrete mixture. The mobility of the concrete mixture is determined by the size of the slump (in *cm) of* a standard concrete cone (truncated cone with a height of 30 *cm, the* diameter of the lower base is 20 cm, the upper base is 10 cm). Stiffness is established by a simplified method of Prof. B. G. Skramtaev or with the help of a technical ***viscometer*** and is expressed by the time in a second required to transform the cone from the concrete mixture into an equal-sized prism or cylinder. After compaction of the latter, the mold is removed. The resulting cone of concrete mixture settles under its own weight.

The value of the cone settlement (cm) serves as an estimate of the mobility of the concrete mixture. According to this indicator, mixtures are distinguished: cast - with a cone slump of more than 12 cm, mobile: 4 - 12 cm, low-mobility: 2- 4 cm, stiff and especially stiff: 0 cm.

Figure 1. Standard cone for determining the mobility of the concrete mixture

These tests are performed on a standard laboratory vibration platform with an automatic switch, which is also used in the production of control samples. The choice of concrete mixture by the degree of its mobility or stiffness is made depending on the type of structure to be concreted, methods of transportation and placement of concrete.

The plastic expressiveness of structures and sculpture made of concrete is enhanced by its porous, light-absorbing surface, and the rich gradation of decorative properties of B. is used in interior decoration and decorative art.

Concrete strength is the most important property of *concrete*. The main quality indicators of heavy concrete are compressive and tensile strength, frost resistance and water resistance. The strength of concrete at the design age is characterized by compressive and axial tensile strength classes. A distinctive feature of concrete works is the significant heterogeneity of the resulting concrete. The higher the culture of construction, the better the quality of preparation and placement of concrete in the structure, the less fluctuations in strength. Consequently, it is important not only to obtain concrete of a given average strength, but also to ensure it in the entire volume of manufactured structures.

The *concrete class* is an indicator that takes into account possible variations in quality. Concrete class is a numerical characteristic of a concrete property, which is taken with a guaranteed security (usually 0.95). This means that the property set by the class, e.g. concrete strength, is achieved in at least 95 out of 100 cases. The concept of **"concrete class"** allows the strength to be assigned with taking into account its actual or possible variation. According to GOST the following classes of heavy concrete in compressive strength are established: B3,5; B5; B7,5; B10; B12,5; B15; B20; B25; B30; B35; B40; B40; B45; B50; B55; B60; B65; B70; B75 and B80. Class of concrete for compressive strength is denoted by the Latin letter B, to the right of which attribute its strength in MPa. Thus, the concrete class B15 compressive strength limit - not less than 15 MPa with a guaranteed security of 0.95. Where necessary, concrete classes are also established for axial tensile strength, denoted by the index B_t, and for flexural tensile strength - B_{tb}.

Concrete performs much worse in tension than in compression: the tensile strength is 10...20 times less than the compressive strength. To increase the load-bearing capacity, especially in bending and tension, concrete is combined with steel reinforcement to produce reinforced concrete structures.

Concrete grade is a numerical characteristic of any of its properties, calculated as the average of the results of testing samples. When determining grades for strength, frost resistance, water resistance, the lower limit value of properties is taken, and the grade for average density is determined by the upper limit value. In contrast to the class, the concrete grade does not take into account the strength fluctuations in the entire volume of the concreted structure.

Compressive strength grade is the most common characteristic of concrete. *The grade is determined by* axial compression testing of concrete cube specimens with dimensions 15x15x15 cm in the established design age (usually 28 days). The compressive strength obtained during the test as the arithmetic mean of the two largest (in a series of three samples), expressed in kgf/cm^2, is a numerical characteristic of the grade.

The following grades of heavy concrete by compressive strength are established: M50; M75; M100; M150; M200; M250, MZOO; M350; M400; M450; M500; M550; M600; M700; M800; M900 and M1000. The index "M" is used in the designation. For example, the concrete grade M200 means that its compressive strength is not less than 200 kgf/cm^2. The relationship between classes and grades of concrete is ambiguous and depends on the homogeneity of concrete, assessed using the *coefficient of variation.* The smaller the coefficient of variation, the more homogeneous the concrete. The class of concrete of the same grade increases significantly if the coefficient of variation is reduced. For example, with a compressive strength grade of M300 and a coefficient of variation of 18%, concrete of class B15 is obtained, and with a coefficient of variation of 5% - class B20, i.e. a whole step higher.

Portland cement concrete gains strength gradually. At normal temperature and constant moisture content, concrete strength growth continues for a long time, but the rate of strength gain fades with time.

Table 3

Ratio between grades and classes of heavy concrete in terms of compressive strength

Concrete class	Concrete grade	Concrete class	Concrete grade
B3.5	M50	B35	M450
B5	M75	B40	M500
B7.5	M100	B45	M600
B10	M150	B50	M700
B12.5	M150	B55	M700
B15	M200	B60	M800
B20	M250	B65	M900
B25	M350	B70	M900
B30	M400	B75	M1000
		B80	M1000

There are correlations between the class and its average strength at an endowment factor of 1 = 0.95:

$$B = I\text{-}0.778 \text{ or } K = B / 0.778$$

When designing structures, the concrete class is most often assigned, and in some cases the concrete grade is assigned. The ratio of classes and grades for heavy concrete in terms of compressive strength is given in Table 3.

The strength of concrete depends on the B/C. With decreasing B/C it increases, with increasing it decreases. In order to obtain a workable concrete mixture, usually 40-70% of water is introduced (B/C=0.4...0.7) Excessive water forms pores in concrete, which reduce its strength.

At B/C from 0.4 to 0.7 (C/V=2.5...1.43) between concrete strength R_b (MPa), cement activity $R_{(ts)}$ (MPa), and C/V there is a linear relationship expressed by the formula:

$$R_b = LR_{(ts)} (Ts/B - 0.5) \quad (1)$$

At B/C < 0.4 (C/v > 2.5) the linear dependence is broken. However, in practical calculations another linear dependence is used:

$$R_b = L1\ R_{(ts)} - (Ts/V + 0.5) \quad (2)$$

The error in calculations in this case does not exceed 2 - 4 %.

A, A_1 - coefficients taking into account the quality of materials. For high-quality materials A=0.65, A1=0.43, for ordinary materials - A=0.50, A_1=0.4; for low-quality materials - A=0.55, A_1=0.37.

In hardened concrete, pores are formed by water which has not hydrated with cement and which has been introduced to make the concrete mix workable. Porosity P (%), is determined by the formula:

$$P = [(B - \omega C) / 100] \times 100 \quad (3)$$

where B and C are water and cement content, kg/m^3;

ω - chemically bound water, its quantity is taken as 0.2.

Reduce porosity and, accordingly, increase the density of concrete can be lowered B / C, the use of alumina, expanding and pozzolanic with denser cement stone, quality compaction of the concrete mixture, the creation of favorable temperature and humidity conditions of curing. The density of concrete determines its strength, water resistance and durability.

The water permeability of concrete is the ability of *concrete* not to allow water to pass through under pressure. It is important for hydraulic structures, water storage tanks. According to the degree of water resistance concrete is divided into grades W2, W4, W6, [1]#8, W10, W12, W14, W16, W18 and [1]#20. The numbers 2-20 denote the pressure in kgf/cm^2 at which standard concrete specimens with a diameter and height of 15 cm do not allow water to pass through them.

Frost resistance is the ability of water-saturated concrete to retain strength and not collapse under alternate freezing and thawing. The cause of destruction is the property of water at the transition to ice to increase in volume by more than 9% and create internal pressure on the walls of pores. According to frost resistance concrete is divided into grades T50, T75, P100, P150, T200, T300, T400, 500, T600, T800 and T1000. The grade is assigned depending on the type of structures and conditions of their operation. Heavy concrete by degree of frost resistance is divided into grades from T50 to T700. For the preparation of frost-resistant concrete is recommended to use Portland cement and its varieties: plasticized, hydrophobic, quick-hardening and sulfate-resistant. The permissible amount of three-calcium aluminate C_3

A in the clinker for Portland cement, depending on the grade of concrete for frost resistance should be, %: for concrete grade B300 and above - no more than 5%, for B200 - no more than 7%, for P100 - no more than 10%. It is not recommended to introduce active mineral additives in cement, which increase the water consumption of the binder in concrete. In order to reduce the water consumption of the concrete mixture and reduce the proportion of micropores in the concrete should be used additives of surfactants that have an air-involving, microgas-forming, hydrophobizing or plasticizing effect on the concrete mixture. For hydraulic structures with standardized frost resistance B200 and above the volume of the involved air at a maximum aggregate size of 20 mm and B / C = 0,41 ... 0,5 should be 2 ... 4 %. Frost-resistant concrete can be obtained by ensuring accurate dosage of the constituent materials, thorough mixing, compaction and proper care of the hardening concrete. Care must be taken to avoid destructive processes during heat treatment of the concrete due to thermal expansion of the constituents, water and air in the freshly placed concrete. In the manufacture of concrete and reinforced concrete structures of increased frost resistance (P200), natural conditions at positive temperature and preservation of its moisture state for 10 days at the same time are preferable for concrete curing.

Shrinkage and expansion. When curing in air, concrete (unless it is based on shrinkage-free or expanding cements) shrinks, and when curing in damp conditions it may swell slightly. The shrinkage value of heavy concrete is usually about 0.15 mm per 1 m of length of the concrete structure, which may entail the formation of cracks in massive and larger structures. When concreting massive structures in the first period of hardening of concrete, it is possible that it expands due to heating by the heat generated by the interaction of cement and water. In order to reduce the heat release of concrete it is necessary to use cements with low exothermia, as well as to arrange temperature joints. Concretes on hydraulic binders (except for concretes on shrinkage-free and expanding cements) are confirmed to shrink when curing in air and decrease in volume. When curing in water, the volume of concrete increases slightly at the beginning, swelling occurs, and then shrinkage occurs when curing in air. The alternating wetting and drying of concrete leads to alternating swelling and shrinkage, and the swelling strain is much smaller than the shrinkage strain. These processes are observed as a result of volumetric changes in the cement stone. Shrinkage has a damping character. It is most significant in the first day of curing. All shrinkage in concrete on ordinary Portland cement is 0.3-0.5mm per 1m length. It increases with the increase in cement consumption, fineness of its grinding, use of belite cements, and aggregates reduce the shrinkage of concrete. Shrinkage deformations lead to cracks in concrete and reduce its durability. Alternate moistening and drying loosen the structure of concrete.

Creep of concrete is manifested by the occurrence of residual deformations under prolonged exposure to a constant load. It occurs as a result of the occurrence and development of microcracks and plastic properties of the cement gel. Creep causes relaxation of stresses, which equalize in non-uniformly loaded areas (this is a positive action). In prestressed structures there is stress loss of reinforcement. Here the negative action of creep is manifested. Creep of concrete subsides after several years of operation of structures.

The thermal conductivity of heavy concrete is 1.28-1.74 W/(m-^{0}C). It increases with increasing average density and moisture content of concrete.

Fire resistance is the property of concrete to retain high temperatures during short-term exposure to fire. It depends on the type of materials used. Destruction of Portland cement occurs at a temperature of 500-550^{0}C as a result of decomposition of calcium hydroxide according to the following scheme

$$Ca\,(OH)_{(2)} = Ca + H_2\,O.$$

Already heating at temperatures between 100 and 2500C reduces the strength of Portland cement concrete by 25%. And yet concrete is a fire-resistant material. Its heating rate is low. It has low thermal conductivity, and much of the heat is spent on evaporation of chemically bound water released during the destruction of cement stone. It resists short-term high temperatures well. If the structure is subjected to high temperatures for a long period of time, heat-resistant concrete should be used. Concrete is a fire-resistant material. However, prolonged exposure to temperatures in the range of 160 -200°C reduces the strength of concrete by 25-30%. When heated above 500°C, concrete is destroyed. Structures exposed to temperatures above 200°C should be protected with heat-insulating materials or made of heat-resistant concrete.

Methodological instructions for the lecture. It is necessary to pay attention to the factors affecting the strength of concrete. Know the differences between the class (B) and grade (M) of concrete and the basic properties of concrete: strength, plasticity and mobility, water resistance, frost resistance, thermal conductivity, fire resistance.

Questions to check theoretical knowledge of the lecture

1. What factors affect the strength of concrete?
2. What is the difference between class and grade of concrete?
3. How is the strength of concrete determined?
4. What is the grade of concrete?
5. What is a brand?
6. Give a definition of the basic properties of concrete.

CHAPTER 3. CALCULATION OF MATERIALS COSTS FOR 1m^3 OF BETON MIX

Purpose: To determine the consumption of materials (Portland cement, water, sand, crushed stone or gravel) per 1m^3 of concrete mix.

The quantity of ingredients used is always greater than the volume of the total product. When reinforcement is placed, only high-grade concrete grades should be used. Naturally, the material consumption will increase in this case. To calculate the material consumption of a particular volume of concrete, it is required to take into account the exact weight of the cement mortar. The consumption of crushed stone is acceptable with an error of 5 kg. This calculation is required to more accurately determine the strength factor of the material. Thus, its future stiffness and fluidity are determined. It is well known from practice that the strength of concrete depends on the amount of cement mortar used. The less cement used, the stronger it becomes. Before calculating the required volume, it is necessary to find out what brand of cement is most suitable for the object. To make the consumption more economical, it is necessary that the grade of cement is greater than the grade of concrete. With a lower grade, the cost of concrete mortar at the output will be very high. It should be noted that the material consumption in this case will turn out to be very high.

The composition of a concrete mixture is expressed as a ratio by weight (less often by volume - less precise) between the quantities of cement, sand and crushed stone (or gravel) with an indication of the water-cement ratio. The amount of cement is taken as a unit. Therefore, in general, the composition of the concrete mixture is expressed by the ratio cement) : P(pe$_{OOK}$) : P(crushed stone), e.g. 1:2.4:4.5 at B/C=0.45. There are 2 concrete compositions: nominal (laboratory), taken for materials in dry condition, and production (field) - for materials with natural moisture.

Calculation of concrete composition is made in the following order: determine the water-cement ratio, which provides concrete of a given strength and water consumption; calculate the required consumption of cement, and then crushed stone (or gravel) and sand; check the mobility (stiffness) of the concrete mixture in case of deviation of these indicators from the project; prepare samples to determine the strength and test in a given time; recalculate the nominal composition of the concrete mixture on the production. The methodology of calculating the composition of concrete will be considered in practical classes.

Many people who build a house on their own, it is very important to know what will be the consumption of materials per $1m^3$ of concrete. Before calculating the required volume, it is necessary to find out what grade of cement is most suitable for this object. In order for the consumption to be more economical, it is necessary that the grade of cement is greater than the grade of concrete. If the grade is lower, the cost of the concrete mortar will be very high.

The consumption of construction material per $1m^3$ of quality ready-mix concrete may vary depending on the nature of the structure. For example, complex building elements, such as capital slabs, require a different composition (1 part cement and 2 parts sand). For structures that will not be subjected to heavy loads (sidewalks, walkways), the mixture is prepared at the rate of one measure of cement to five measures of sand. The amount of crushed stone should reach 70% of the total volume of the obtained material.

First of all, it is necessary to determine which cement grade is best to use on each individual site. To ensure economical consumption, it is recommended to choose a cement grade that exceeds the grade of the future concrete. Otherwise, the price of the construction mixture at the output will be significantly overestimated, and the material will be of low quality. If special strength is not needed, the mixture is added:

- sand;
- stone meal.

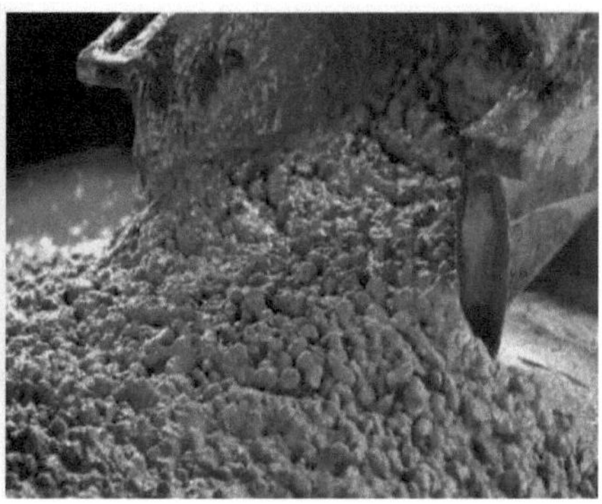

The water-cement ratio for a quality mortar is determined by its grade and the curing time of the screed. The most durable concrete in private construction is M500, and the ratio of cement to sand is made at the rate of 1:3. To obtain a high-quality solution, it is necessary to strictly observe the norms of consumption of materials required for the manufacture of 1 $m^{(3)\ of}$ concrete. More details about them you will learn below. If there is a significant error with an insufficient amount of cement, the connection between the ingredients will be broken, as a result of which, under load, the structure will collapse very quickly. It can be damaged even when exposed to adverse weather conditions or aggressive climate.

Calculation of materials for the preparation of 1 m3 of concrete directly depends on its grade, the choice of which, in turn, is determined by the destination. In individual construction of small buildings, concrete M200 is most often used, which is characterized by good compressive strength. To create a high-quality mixture of M200 we need cement of brand M400. Such a solution is poured:

- foundations;
- of the grounds;
- garden and park paths;
- stairs;
- concrete pads.

Experienced builders advise to prepare a small amount of concrete at home in order to experimentally find out the necessary density. In addition, the peculiarity of mortar materials is that they set very quickly, so a large volume of the mixture may simply not have time to work out. To prevent technological voids from forming in the finished construction elements after curing, gravel of different caliber should be used.

The tables below show the consumption of each material per $1m^3$ of concrete, depending on the concrete grade:

cement (Table 4),

water (Table 5):

sand and crushed stone (Table 6).

Table 4

Cement consumption

Type of construction	Concrete grade	Cement grade	Consumption, kg
Simple products	M100	300/400	225
Reinforced concrete products	M150 - M300	300 - 600	265 - 380
Reinforced sections	M400/M500	600	480 - 530

Make sure that the screed water is clean and free of suspended solids (silt, algae, dirt). On the amount of water depends on the plasticity index of concrete and its strength after setting. Remember that it is much easier to add water than bulk components, so pour the liquid gradually. The smaller the size of the mortar ingredients, the greater will be the water consumption in each cube of the mixture. Stiff concrete is easy to identify by its appearance. To do this, a small amount of viscous mass is placed on the shovel, which should not spread on the surface.

Table 5

Water consumption

Concrete grade	Cement grade	B/C ratio
100	200, 250, 300	0.68, 0.75, 0.8
150	200, 250, 300, 400, 500, 600	0.5, 0.57, 0.66, 0.7, 0.72. 0.75
200	200, 250, 300, 400, 500, 600	0.35, 0.43, 0.53, 0.58, 0.64, 0.66
250	200, 250, 300, 400, 500, 600	0.25, 0.36, 0.42, 049, 0.56, 0.6
300	250, 300, 400, 500, 600	0.28, 0.35, 0.42, 0.49 0.54
400	400, 500, 600	0.33, 0.38, 0.46

Now it is possible to determine the amount of sand and crushed stone per m^3 of mortar of different grades. To do this, the volumes of water and cement must be subtracted from one cube. The final sum and will determine the proportion of sand and fillers. It should be noted that the ratio of ingredients is affected by the coarseness of sand, and this is necessarily taken into account when mixing quality mortar.

Table 6

Crushed stone and sand consumption

Crushed stone, mm	Sand, %	Water, ml/m^3
10	56	230
15	52	220
20	49	200
25	46	195
40	41	185
50	39	177
70	35	167

The normal size of the sand grain, which is included in the mortar, is considered to be 3.5 mm. In addition, the sand should not have impurities of clay, from which the mixture may lose its strength. Now we know what you need to pay attention to in the first place to get a quality product that meets all the requirements of modern construction.

Methodological instructions for the lecture. It is necessary to know the sequence of calculation of concrete mixture by ratios between the amounts of cement, sand, crushed stone or gravel by weight.

Questions to check theoretical knowledge of the lecture

1. What is the order in which the concrete composition is calculated?
2. How is the water flow rate determined?
3. What formula is used to determine cement consumption?
4. How is the coarse aggregate consumption determined?
5. Which formula is used to determine the consumption of fine aggregate?

CHAPTER 4. PECULIARITIES OF CONCRETING IN WINTER TIME

Purpose: To train the student in winter concreting techniques.

Concreting in winter time is associated with certain peculiarities. It should be understood that the rate of concrete hardening at subzero temperatures is significantly reduced, so before diluting the additives and water for the future mortar must be heated.

The temperature of the water and concrete components at the time of loading into the mixer shall be such as to ensure that the specified temperature regime is obtained when the resulting mortar leaves the mixer.

When the temperature of concrete drops below +5^{0}C, its hardening and strength gain slow down sharply, and at temperatures equal to the freezing point it practically stops. At sub-zero temperatures, water in freshly placed concrete can also freeze. At the same time, not only the hardening of the concrete stops, but also under the influence of ice can begin to destroy the weak structure of the concrete. After thawing and further curing, such concrete will have a reduced strength, which is explained by the ice crystals breaking the bonds between the granular aggregate and cement stone.

The following mistakes often occur during winter concreting:

- increases the time required to finish the concrete surface;
- increase in the cost of concreting;
- a weak dusty concrete surface is formed;
- cracks are forming.

To avoid the above consequences, the following recommendations should be adhered to during the preparation and placement of the concrete mixture.

When pouring concrete in winter, it is necessary to remember about the need to maintain the temperature regime of the concrete mixture:

- freshly prepared concrete mixture must have a temperature not exceeding 30°C;
- concrete mixture when pouring concrete in conditions of average daily air temperature from + 5 ° C to - 3 ° C should have a temperature: for concrete grade from M200 and above

- not less than +5 ° C; for lesser concrete grade - not less than +10 ° C;

- If the air temperature is below - 3°C, safe concreting is possible if the temperature of the concrete mixture is maintained at a level not lower than + 10°C for 3 days.

Concrete heating station SPB-35 Arc

The concrete mix for pouring concrete at low temperatures shall be prepared with the following in mind:

- use a higher cement content;
- reduce the water-cement ratio;
- granular fillers are preheated to + 35°C;
- water is heated to + 70°C;
- heated water is pre-mixed with granular filler and only then cement is added;
- when using a concrete mixer, the ingredients are fed in the following order: granular

aggregate + the main part of heated water; make a few turns; pour the rest of the water. The duration of mixing is at least 1.5-2 minutes (1.5 times longer than according to summer norms);

- use anti-freeze and air-involving additives;
- the concrete mixture is heated to a temperature not exceeding +30°C;
- the duration of vibrating is increased by 1.25 times.

Concrete placed in winter must be protected from freezing during the curing period required to achieve 50% of its design strength. Providing normal curing conditions for concrete in winter is achieved in two ways: using the internal heat of the concrete and additional heat supply to the concrete from outside. Internal heat reserve is created by heating the components of the concrete mixture (water, sand and crushed stone or gravel) in such a way that the temperature of the concrete mixture at the exit from the concrete mixer does not exceed 30 ^{0}C, because at higher temperatures it quickly thickens and loses workability. Water for mixing can be heated up to 80^{0}C, aggregates - up to 40^{0}C. In addition, the heat generated by the chemical reaction of cement with water (cement exotherm) prevents the structure from cooling. In order to keep the heat reserve for a certain period of time, concrete mix structures are covered with thermal insulating materials. The thickness of the coating is determined by a thermal engineering calculation. This method is called "thermos". It is used for concreting massive structures having a surface modulus (ratio of concrete surface cooling to volume) not more than 6. In thin structures, and sometimes in massive ones, the freshly placed concrete mixture is heated by steam or electric current (electric heating). Steam for heating concrete with a temperature of 50 - 80^{0}C is usually introduced into the gaps between the walls of double formwork or in channels cut from the inside of the formwork; sometimes it is passed through pipes laid inside the concrete. This method makes it possible to obtain in 1 - 2 days the strength equal to 60 - 70% of the strength (28-day).

Concrete is electrically heated with alternating current. The current is transmitted by electrodes of two types: surface electrodes (in the form of steel plates laid on the surface) and internal electrodes (in the form of steel rods laid horizontally or vertically). When making a reinforced concrete structure, rebar is used as one of the electrodes. When an electric current passes through concrete, heat is released, causing the concrete to heat up and harden quickly.

However, the concrete to be heated must not exceed a temperature of 60^{0}°C. Otherwise, the concrete may dry out locally.

The concrete mixture is heated during the concrete preparation process. The heating temperature is selected depending on the duration and method of concrete transportation to the place of placement and the ambient air temperature. It is important that by the time the monolithic concrete structure is completed, the temperature in the concrete body does not fall below $+15^{0}$C. After placing the concrete mixture, the structure is covered with insulating material so that the concrete hardens at a positive temperature. Concreting of massive monolithic structures is carried out taking into account the temperature released during cement hydration. To determine the exact temperature inside the curing concrete, temperature sensors are placed in the concrete.

Structural heating. Electric and infrared heating is used to raise the temperature in the concrete body. It is necessary to take into account the fact that the normal temperature for the hardening of concrete is considered to be $+15^{0}$C +20 ° C. If the temperature is reduced, the hardening of the solution slows down, and at zero degrees Celsius and stops altogether. Special anti-freeze additives in concrete can remedy the situation, which allow the mortar to be used even at sub-zero temperatures.

The use of *antifreeze additives* is used to prevent freezing of concrete during transportation and placement of concrete mix. As antifreeze additives for the preparation of concrete are used:

- calcium chloride (CC);
- calcium nitrate (NC);
- a mixture consisting of calcium nitrite and calcium nitrate (NNK);
- a mixture of nitrite, nitrate and calcium chloride (NNHC);
- sodium chloride (SC);
- sodium nitrite (SN);
- sodium sulfate (CH);
- Urea (urea);

- potash (P);
- sodium formate;
- filtrate of technical pentaerythritol.

CC and CH are the most effective anti-freeze additives. At the same time, they can cause corrosion of reinforcement and form efflorescence (white scale) on the surface. Therefore, their use is strictly limited. Concrete mixtures with low dosages of HC and sodium formate can be used at ambient temperatures down to -20^0C without fear of corrosion of reinforcement and the appearance of efflorescence on the surface of the concrete.

Antifreeze additives perform two functions at once: they reduce the hardening of concrete and at the same time lower the freezing point of water. The water remains in liquid form, allowing concrete to harden even at temperatures below freezing.

Methodological instructions for the lecture. It is necessary to know the ways to ensure normal conditions of concrete curing in winter, as well as ways to protect concrete from freezing in winter.

Questions to test theoretical knowledge

What are some ways to ensure normal curing conditions for concrete in winter?

1. Name the methods of winter concreting.
2. What is the surface modulus of concrete?
3. Which concrete structures are classified as massive?
4. What anti-freeze additives are used?

CHAPTER 5. SPECIAL TYPES OF HEAVY CONCRETES

Objective: to familiarize with special types of concrete and their applications.

High-strength concrete with a strength of 60... 100 MPa is obtained on the basis of cement of high grades, washed sand and crushed stone with strength not lower than 100 MPa. High-strength concrete is prepared with low B/C = 0.3...0.35 (mixtures are stiff or low-moving) in compulsory concrete mixers. For placing mixtures and molding products use intensive compaction: vibrating with a load, double vibrating, etc. A significant effect in the production of high-strength concrete give superplasticizers.

As a rule, high-strength concretes are also quick-hardening, however, in order to achieve the tempering strength of the products in a short period of time, heat treatment under a reduced regime is used. New especially quick-hardening cements make it possible to produce concrete products without heat treatment. Heavy concrete has high tensile strength, wear and frost resistance. To prepare high-strength concrete, all means are used, such as: take extremely low water-cement ratio, superplasticizers, high-strength cement, thorough mixing and compaction of the concrete mixture and strict care of the concrete.

Hydrotechnical concrete refers to concrete used for the construction of hydraulic structures (dams, water-regulating, water intake and other structures).

Concretes for transportation construction are designed for the construction of bridges, overpasses, overpasses, culverts and regulation structures on railways and roads.

Road concrete is referred to heavy concrete. It is used in the construction of highways and airfields. By purpose it is divided into concrete for single-layer pavements, for the top and bottom layers of two-layer pavements, as well as for the bases of improved pavements. Road concrete is subject to requirements for compressive strength, flexural tensile strength, frost resistance, abrasion resistance. High durability of concrete is achieved by the standardization of B/C, which is accepted for the concrete of one-layer and the top layer of two-layer pavements not higher than 0.5. For the bottom layer, working in more favorable conditions, B/C = 0.6 and higher. For bases of improved pavements B/C of concrete mixtures is not standardized. The workability of the concrete mixture is 2 - 4cm. Although in recent years there is experience of laying stiff mixtures with compaction with rollers. The durability of concrete depends on the quality of materials. Portland cements without mineral additives with SZA content up to 8%, plasticized and hydrophobic cements or PVA should be used in concrete mixtures. Sand and coarse aggregate should be of high quality.

Heat-resistant called *concrete* capable of maintaining long-term strength at temperatures above 2000C; use hydraulic binders: Portland cement, quick-hardening Portland cement, slag Portland cement, alumina, high alumina and barium cements; air binders - liquid sodium glass, periclase cement; chemical: silicate - clay, phosphate compounds. Fillers are crushed stone and sand obtained from burnt clay, refractory and refractory products, from secondary materials - blast-furnace, fuel, ferrochrome and other slags; rocks - quartzite, basalt, diabase, tuff, volcanic slag, pumice. Specially manufactured porous artificial aggregates are also used - expanded clay, aglopyrite, shungizite, perlite, vermiculite, etc. In order to increase the resistance of concrete when heated, finely ground additives from chromite ore, fireclay, magnesite bricks, andesite, granulated blast furnace slag, etc. are introduced into its composition. The fineness of grinding of the admixture for concrete on Portland cement should be such that through the sieve number 009 passed not less than 70%, and for concrete on liquid glass - not less than 50%. As fine and coarse aggregate used chromite, fireclay, clay brick slaughter, basalt, diabase, andesite and others. With properly selected binders and aggregates concrete can withstand for a long time, without breaking down, the effect of temperature up to 1200 ° C. The choice of materials is made depending on the temperature conditions of its operation. Heat-resistant concrete on Portland cement and alumina cement produced class (grade) not less than B20 (250), and on liquid glass - B 12.5 (150). Concretes on liquid glass are not used in conditions of frequent exposure to water, and on Portland cement - in conditions of acidic aggressive environment. For heat-resistant concretes operated at a temperature of 800 ° C, determine the residual strength after heating them at this temperature. For concretes used at 600 and 700°C, the specimens are heated to this temperature and then the residual strength is determined. The durability of heat resistant concrete is evaluated by their thermal resistance. Usually Portland cement concrete is used in structures at temperatures up to 200^0C. It should be taken into account that the compressive strength of concrete is reduced by 25%. Concretes on Portland cement of different compositions are used in one-sided heating with a limiting temperature of 1700 ° C, on alumina cement and liquid glass - up to 1400 ° C. Heat-resistant concretes are used for manufacturing various thermal units and chimneys.

Structural - heat-insulating concretes are designed for reinforced concrete structures, which are subject to requirements both in terms of load-bearing capacity and heat-insulating properties.

Corrosion-resistant concrete is concrete capable of resisting the action of aggressive media under operating conditions.

Special types of concrete also include fine-grained concrete, cast-in-place concrete, decorative concrete, and concrete for radiation protection.

Fine-grained concrete is concrete with aggregate size up to 10 mm. Fine-grained concrete can be placed by shotcrete with the help of a cement gun. The cement gun is filled with a dry mixture of fine-grained concrete, which is supplied by compressed air through a flexible hose to the place of concrete placement. To the outlet of the flexible hose through a special hose under pressure comes in the right amount of water. At the nozzle outlet, the dry mix is wetted with water and applied to the concrete surface in its finished form. This method of placing concrete mixture produces fine-grained concrete of high density, strength, frost resistance and water resistance. There is also a conventional method, i.e. laying the ready-mix in a formwork or mold with subsequent compaction and heat treatment (if necessary), used in the arrangement of impervious linings of channels and ponds in the construction of various containers, in the manufacture of thin-walled panels and paving slabs, sealing expansion joints of hydraulic structures, etc. Fine-grained concrete is characterized by a high content of cement stone, so its shrinkage and creep are somewhat higher. It is used in the manufacture of thin-walled, including reinforced cement structures, as well as in cases where there is no coarse aggregate. The properties of fine-grained concrete are characterized by the same factors as conventional concrete. However, the absence of coarse aggregate leads to an increase in water consumption of the concrete mixture, and to obtain equal-strength concrete and equal-slip mixture increases cement consumption by 20...40% To reduce cement consumption it is necessary to use high-quality sands, plasticizing additives, superplasticizers, to produce a good compaction of the mixture. Fine-grained concrete has increased flexural strength, good water and frost resistance.

Cast concrete is expedient to use in hydraulic engineering construction for concreting thin-walled densely reinforced structures with complex configuration, where laying and vibration of conventional mixtures is difficult, as well as in the concreting of monolithic lining of construction irrigation canals of various cross-sections and production of precast concrete for land reclamation construction. Cast concrete mix is prepared from cement, sand with the content of fine particles (finer than 0.15 mm) up to 15% of the mass of coarse aggregate, water-retaining additives (concrete clay, etc.), microfillers (fly ash, expanded clay dust, etc.). Concrete mixture for cast-in-place concrete is obtained cast (flowable), which allows its placement without mechanical impact.

Concrete for protection against radioactive effects - these are especially heavy concretes, protect against cement - rays and neutron radiation, which pose the greatest danger to living organisms during nuclear decay. Portland cement, slag-portland cement, alumina cement, etc. serve as binders. As additional aggregates are used materials of increased density - barite, limonite, magnesite, cast iron scrap, steel scraps, on which it is possible to obtain concrete with average density from 2800 to 5000kg/m^3. To improve their properties, additives of boron carbide, lithium chloride, cadmium sulfate, containing light elements - hydrogen, lithium, cadmium, boron - are introduced into their composition. As aggregates for such concrete are used materials with high density - barite, magnetite, limonite, as well as metal scrap in the form of cast iron shot, scraps of reinforcing strip and profile metal, metal shavings and others. The density of protective especially heavy concrete depends on the type of aggregate and its density. Portland cement, slag-portland cement and alumina cement are used as binders for the preparation of especially heavy concrete. In special concretes, the most effective binder may be a substance which, as a result of hardening, attaches a large amount of water (in order to increase the hydrogen in the concrete). Such a substance is calcium hydrosulfoaluminate, which is formed by the interaction of tris-calcium aluminate contained in Portland cement with gypsum. Therefore, one type of special purpose cement contains elevated amounts of tricalcium aluminate and gypsum. To prevent its possible spontaneous destruction, hydraulic additives (trepel, diatomite, etc.) are added to it. In addition to Portland cement, alumina, expanding and shrinkage-free cements are also used. But the latter binders have a high cost. To improve the protective properties of hydrate concretes (these concretes received this name for their high water content), additives are introduced to increase the content of hydrogen, carbide, boron, lithium chloride, cadmium sulfate, and other additives containing light elements - hydrogen, lithium, cadmium and boron-containing substances.

Acid-resistant concrete is produced using acid-resistant cement and acid-resistant aggregates. The concrete mixture is filled with soluble glass in an amount that provides the necessary mobility of the concrete mixture. For the manufacture of acid-resistant concrete with resistance to the action of inorganic acids (except hydrofluoric), use a mixture of soluble glass (sodium silicate) with 15% sodium silicofluoride KhaHyЪ, as well as quartz sand, crushed stone from Beshtownite, andesite or quartzite and dust-like fraction (finer than 0.15 mm), prepared from acid-resistant materials. Curing of acid-resistant concrete should take place in a warm, air-dry environment. Acid-resistant concrete is characterized by a strong bond with steel reinforcement, resistance to the action of sulfuric, hydrochloric, nitric acids, etc. (except for hydrofluoric acid). (except hydrofluoric acid), compressive strength in 3 days - 11...12 MPa, in 28 days - 15 MPa. Under the action of water and weak acids acid-resistant concrete is gradually destroyed, the action of concentrated acids this concrete resists well, but alkali solutions easily destroy it. Acid-resistant concrete is used for various structures and lining of equipment in the chemical industry, replacing expensive materials: sheet lead, acid-resistant ceramics, hewn stone.

Decorative concretes are used for architectural finishing of structural elements of buildings and structures - walls, floors, staircases, separating strips of road surfaces, etc. They are composed of colored or white cements, *pigments* and colored aggregates. Their composition includes colored or white cements, pigments and colored aggregates. Pigments should be alkali - and light-resistant. They may be added not more than 8 - 10% of the cement weight. Usually Portland cements with pigments are used for dark-colored concrete, white - for light-colored concrete. Fillers are made of colored rocks: marble, red and pink granite, syenite, labradorite and others. To obtain a texture that meets the architectural design, the surface of the aggregates exposed by grinding, chipping mills. Decorative concrete is obtained by introducing into the concrete mixture of alkali and light-resistant pigments in the amount of 8...10 % of the weight of cement (ochre, mummy, dusting, etc.) or the use of colored cements. In some cases, aggregates with the necessary color are used, for example, tuffs, red quartzite, marble and other colored rocks. Colored concretes are used for decorative purposes in the construction of buildings and structures, in the construction of crosswalks, dividing strips on road surfaces, parkways, as well as the manufacture of elements of urban landscaping, for exterior decoration of buildings, should be durable.

Methodological instructions for the lecture. It is necessary to know the types of special concretes, materials for their preparation and areas of application.

Theoretical knowledge control questions

1. What special types of heavy concrete do you know?
2. Where are cast-in-place and fine-grained concrete used?
3. Name the properties of heat resistant concrete?
4. For what finishes of structural elements of buildings and constructions are decorative concretes used?
5. What additional aggregates are used in concrete to protect against radiation?

CHAPTER 6. LIGHTWEIGHT CONCRETE

Objective: to familiarize with varieties and properties of lightweight concrete in the field of their application, materials for the manufacture of lightweight concrete.

Lightweight concrete, characterized by high porosity (up to 40%) and relatively low average density (from 500 to 1800 kg/m$^{3)}$, is widely used for the manufacture of load-bearing and enclosing prefabricated concrete and reinforced concrete structures. Their use instead of bricks and heavy concrete makes it possible to increase the heat-protective qualities of enclosures, which, in turn, allows reducing the thickness and weight of building walls and thus reducing transportation costs.

In lightweight concrete as aggregates use sand and crushed stone from pumice, volcanic slag, volcanic tuff, porous limestone and dolomite, limestone - coquina, lime tuff, opoca, trepel, diatomite, fuel slag, porous metallurgical slag, expanded at firing expanded expanded claydite, thermosite, perlite, vermiculite, etc.

Manufacturing. Concrete is made by mixing cement, sand, crushed stone and water (the ratio depends on the cement grade, fraction and moisture content of sand and crushed stone), as well as small amounts of additives (plasticizers, hydrophobizers, etc.). Cement and water are the main binding components in the production of concrete. For example, if 400 grade cement is used to produce 200 grade concrete, a ratio of 1:3:5:0.5 is used. If 500 grade cement is used, this conventional ratio produces 350 grade concrete. The ratio of water to cement ("water-cement ratio", "water-cement modulus"; denoted "W/C") is an important characteristic of concrete. The strength of concrete is directly related to this ratio: the lower the W/C, the stronger the concrete. Theoretically, B/C = 0.2 is sufficient for cement hydration, but the plasticity of such concrete is too low, so in practice B/C = 0.3-0.5 is used.

A common mistake in artisanal concrete production is the excessive addition of water, which increases the mobility of the concrete but reduces its strength several times.

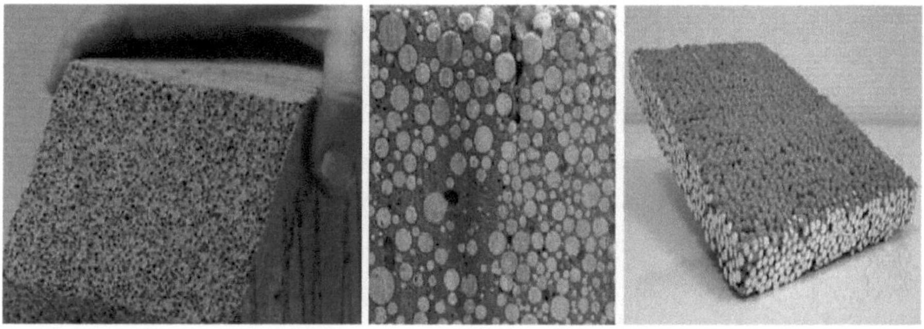

At each stage of construction, different types of light cellular concrete are used. For example, mixtures based on expanded clay are used for foundation or flooring, walls are laid with building blocks made of foam or aerated concrete, arbolite, slag, etc. The insulation of slabs made of lightweight concrete can be done with polystyrene concrete. Insulate slabs of lightweight concrete can be insulated with polystyrene concrete. The structure resembles a natural material - pumice.

Gost establishes the composition of the mixture, which is the determinant for this concrete, particularly in terms of aggregates.

1. Using one type of mineral porous aggregate (expanded clay, vermiculite, agloporite, perlite) or two (expanded clay-vermiculite concrete, expanded clay-perlite concrete);

2. With organic aggregates (polystyrene concrete or PSFB, arbolite, pumice or tuff concrete).

Depending on the type of coarse aggregate used, lightweight concrete is divided into expanded clay concrete, agloporite concrete, slag concrete, pumice concrete, etc.

According to the structure of the concrete under consideration are divided into the following main types: ordinary lightweight concrete, made of binder, water, fine and coarse aggregates, with the solution completely filling the voids between the grains of coarse aggregate. The amount of air involved in the concrete mixture does not exceed 6% of the volume; large-porous (sandless) lightweight concrete, in which the grains of coarse aggregate are covered with a thin layer of cement batter, and the intergranular voids remain free. The coarse porous structure contains more than 25% of the voids filled with air; porous lightweight concretes based on a binder and a pore-forming agent, in the structure of which air cells occur. This increases the porosity of the cement mortar and thus reduces the density of the concrete.

By purpose lightweight concrete on porous aggregates are divided into the following types: insulating - average density in air-dry state less than 500kg/m^3, thermal conductivity not more than 0.25W/(m-(^{0})C), used for the manufacture of insulation boards and other products; structural - insulating with an average density of 500 - 1800kg/m^3, strength not lower than M35, thermal conductivity not more than 0.6W/(m-(^{0})C), used in load-bearing and self-supporting enclosing structures (walls and floors); structural - with average density 1400 - 1800 kg/cm^3, strength not lower than M50, frost resistance B50 and higher, used in load-bearing structures.

According to the type of binder, lightweight concrete is distinguished between cement, lime, gypsum, mixed binder and liquid glass. Portland cement, slag Portland cement, pozzolanic Portland cement, as well as fast hardening Portland cement are used for lightweight concrete non-autoclaved curing.

As aggregates for lightweight concrete are used natural or artificial porous stone materials, on the properties and quality of which depend on the properties of the prepared concrete.

Natural porous aggregates are obtained by crushing and fractionation of porous rocks - pumice, volcanic tuff or lava, limestone - coquina, etc. The most effective among them are pumice and volcanic tuffs, which have high, mainly closed *porosity*, as a result of which their water absorption is small. Among them, the most effective are pumice and volcanic tuffs, which have high, mainly closed, porosity, as a result of which their water absorption is small.

Artificial aggregates are industrial wastes and special processing of natural stone materials. The aggregates that are industrial wastes and are used without preliminary processing include metallurgical and fuel slags, slags of chemical production. The aggregates obtained as a result of special processing of natural stone materials and industrial wastes include expanded clay fired expanded clay expanded clay and agloporite, expanded perlite and vermiculite, granulated slags, ash gravel, etc. The aggregates are used as a result of special processing of natural stone materials and industrial wastes.

Claydite is made from clay raw materials capable of swelling well during the firing process, with an increased content of iron compounds or with additives that release gaseous products. The prepared clay mass is molded into granules, which are dried before firing. The dried granules are fired in rotary kilns at temperatures up to 1200^{0}C. In the process of firing there is a swelling of granules with an increase in their volume by 17 times and the formation of claydite gravel. Varieties of expanded claydite are shungusite, ash gravel, alumina claydite, expanded argillite and trepel, produced by firing with swelling of prepared granules (grains) from clay and sandy-clay rocks (clays, loams, shale, argillite, siltstone), shungite-containing shales, trepels, ash and slag mixture.

Fumed perlite is an artificial porous material obtained from inverted polymineral rocks, which, when heated to 1100 - 13000C, swell and form porous rubble. It is obtained by firing pellets from volcanic rocks (perlite, obsidian and other water-containing volcanic glasses). The process of heat treatment of perlite, depending on the properties of raw materials and the type of finished product (crushed stone and sand) is carried out by one- or two-stage firing in short rotary furnaces and in a suspended state - in vertical furnaces. Perlite crushed stone and sand for concrete has a bulk density of 150 - 450kg/m^3, and perlite sand for thermal insulation backfill -50 - 100kg/m^3.

Bulk vermiculite is a weathering product of natural rock stone (biotite mica), which, when rapidly heated to 700 - 900°C, bulges, increasing in volume by 40 times. It is obtained by firing of prepared grains from natural hydrated layers. From industrial wastes sand and crushed stone are used mainly from granulated or expanded metallurgical slag, as well as coarse-dispersed ashes and ash-and-slag mixtures of thermal power plants.

Agloporite is an artificial porous aggregate with granule size 5 - 20 mm, bulk density 400 - 700 kg/m^3 and strength 0.4 - 1.5 MPa. Raw materials for agloporite are clayey rocks (loam, sandy loam, argillite, clay shale), as well as industrial waste - clay waste from coal mining and preparation, burnt rock, fuel slag, ash from thermal power plants and other stone-like silicate rocks. The technology of production of agloporite gravel from TPP ashes by sintering raw granules on the grids of sintering machines allows to obtain artificial porous aggregate in the form of rounded granules of a certain grain composition with a sintered surface shell of increased strength.

Granulated slag is a fine-grained porous material made by rapid cooling of metallurgical slag melts.

Slag pumice (thermosite) is produced in the form of clumps of cellular structure by swelling of slag melt with the help of water, air or their mixture. Existing methods of porization are divided into two main groups. The first includes methods of melt porization carried out in periodically operating units, for example, in pools; the second includes methods of melt porization in continuously operating units (e.g., hydro-screen unit). Fixation of the porous structure is carried out by rapid cooling of the melt. Pieces of slag pumice are crushed and dispersed into crushed stone and sand. Depending on the bulk density of crushed stone (400 - 800kg/m$^{(3))}$, the strength of the aggregate is 0.4 - 2.0 MPa.

The main properties of lightweight concrete on porous aggregates are density, thermal conductivity, strength and frost resistance. In order to obtain lightweight concrete with given properties, it is necessary not only to choose the initial constituent materials, but also to select the correct concrete composition. The average density of concrete depends mainly on the bulk density and grain size of the aggregate, binder and water consumption.

For the preparation and moistening of lightweight concrete, potable water meeting the same requirements as for heavyweight concrete is used.

Increased porosity of lightweight concrete promotes the occurrence and development of reinforcement corrosion in reinforced concrete products. Therefore, in an aggressive environment, the concrete of a reinforced structure must be dense. As practice shows, in such concrete the cement content should be at least 250kg/m^3. Sometimes the reinforcement is covered with different compositions: cement-casein suspension with sodium nitrite; bituminous mastic with ground sand, ash and solvent - thuol, bituminous cement mastic.

The content of water-soluble sulfur compounds in conversion 804 in aggregates intended for reinforced lightweight concrete shall not exceed 1%, and the softening factor shall not be less than 0.6.

The strength of lightweight concrete depends on the strength of cement stone and aggregates, the strength of which is much lower than the strength of coarse aggregates used in heavyweight concrete. In case of structural reinforcement, lightweight concrete with a dense structure is used. Cement consumption per 1m$^{(3)}$ of concrete mixture in these cases should be at least 200kg per 1m^3. The average density of such concretes is not lower than 800kg/m^3. Such concretes provide good adhesion of the reinforcement to the concrete and reliable protection against corrosion.

The frost resistance of lightweight concrete depends on the type and amount of binder and the frost resistance of the aggregate. Portland cement concrete has a higher frost resistance, which increases with the amount of cement. Frost-resistant lightweight aggregates (pumice, expanded clay, agloporite) allow to obtain concrete with frost resistance B25 - B100. Such concretes are used for external structures of buildings.

Varieties of lightweight concrete:

Cellular concrete is a type of lightweight concrete with evenly distributed pores (up to 85% of the total volume of concrete); it is produced as a result of hardening of a mixture of binder, water and silica component pre-swollen by a pore-forming agent.

According to the type of binder used, cellular concretes are divided into the following groups:

- *gas concrete and foam concrete,* produced on the basis of Portland cement or cement-lime binder;

- *gas silicates and foam silicates*, obtained on the basis of a mixture of lime - boiling lime and quartz sand;

- *gas-slag concretes and foam-slag concretes*, obtained from a mixture of lime and finely ground granulated blast-furnace slags.

According to the conditions of curing differentiate cellular concrete steamed and autoclaved curing.

Foam concrete is prepared by mixing cement batter or mortar with separately prepared stable foam. After hardening of the foam concrete mixture, a concrete of cellular structure is formed. Foam is prepared by vigorously mixing the blowing agent with water. Liquid mixtures of rosin soap and animal glue or an aqueous solution of saponin (extract from plant soap root), as well as the preparation of HA (hydrolyzed blood from the slaughterhouse) are used as a foaming agent. The resulting foam has a stable structure and mixes well with cement dough or mortar. Foam concrete mixture is prepared in foam concrete mixers, then it is poured into metal molds and sent to steaming chambers or autoclaves. In autoclave at temperature 175 - 190^{0}C and steam pressure 0.8 - 1.3 MPa calcium hydroxide intensively interacts with silica component, thus calcium hydrosilicate is formed, which has rather high strength and durability. According to physical and mathematical properties, foam concrete is distinguished:

and) Heat-insulating foam concrete is cast in the form of blocks of size 100x50x50cm and larger, which after curing sawed into slabs, strength up to 2.5 MPa, thermal conductivity 0.1 - 0.2W/(m-°C). This type of foam block is used for thermal insulation of reinforced concrete coverings, partitions, etc;

b) Structural - heat-insulating foam concrete has a strength of 2.57.5MPa, thermal conductivity 0.2-0.4W/(m-^{0}C), it is used for enclosing structures; c) reinforced products for coverings are made of structural foam concrete. They are reinforced with two nets made of wire with a diameter of 3 - 5 mm. Strength up to 2.0 MPa and thermal conductivity 0.4-0.6W/(m-^{0}C), it is widely used in three-layer enclosing structures of heated buildings.

Gas concrete is prepared from a mixture of cement (sometimes with the addition of lime), silica component and water with the introduction of a gas-forming agent - aluminum powder, perehydrol (aqueous solution of hydrogen peroxide H2O2), etc. into the already mixed mixture. The most common gas-forming agent is fine-dispersed aluminum powder (powder). The gassing process occurs as a result of chemical interaction of aluminum with calcium hydroxide. The released hydrogen swells the cement dough, which, when hardened, retains its cellular structure. The initial components of aerated concrete - cement, lime - fluff, ground sand, water - are thoroughly mixed in a mixer, into this solution pour water suspension of aluminum powder and after repeated mixing pour aerated concrete mixture into metal molds, filling them with such a calculation that after the end of bloating form was filled to the top. After aging in the molds, aerated concrete is usually subjected to accelerated curing in autoclaves. Applying autoclave treatment, you can not only provide products with high strength, but also significantly reduce the consumption of cement by partial or replacing it with lime. In the latter case, gas silicates are obtained. Cellular concrete can be drilled and sawed well and can be easily nailed into.

The concrete mixture of large-porous concrete is in most cases prepared from cement, coarse aggregate (crushed stone or gravel) and water. The cement stone connects the individual grains of coarse aggregate along the planes of their contact with each other. Such concrete is called *sandless* concrete. In some cases, a small amount of sand is added to the concrete mixture so that the total volume of cement, sand and water is less than the volume of voids in the coarse aggregate. Such concrete is called *low-sand* concrete. As a coarse aggregate used porous (less often dense) gravel or crushed stone. Cement consumption per $1m^3$ of concrete mixture varies from 70 to 150kg. The coefficient of thermal conductivity of large porous concrete on dense aggregates - from 0.6 to 1 W/(m-K). This is the least efficient lightweight concrete in terms of thermal protection properties. The best heat-protective properties have large-porous concrete on porous aggregates. Since pores are formed in concrete, communicating with each other, for heat protection of premises, the walls of buildings made of large-porous concrete must be plastered on both sides. The grades of large-porous concrete are determined in the same way as for heavy concrete.

Methodological instructions for the lecture. It is necessary to know the basic properties, varieties and applications of lightweight concrete.

Theoretical knowledge control questions

1. What aggregates are used for lightweight concrete?
2. Name the basic properties of lightweight concrete.
3. What does the strength of lightweight concrete depend on?
4. What groups are cellular concrete divided into?
5. What is foam concrete?
6. What is aerated concrete?
7. Why are concretes called sandless and low-sand concrete?

TESTS

1. What kind of stone is concrete?

a)Natural stone from igneous rocks.

b)Natural stone from sedimentary rocks.

c)Artificial stone produced by the hardening of a compacted mixture.

d)Hardened mortar based on mineral binders.

2. Which concretes are extra heavy in terms of average density?

a)$\rho =$ 2500 kg/m^3 and above

b)$\rho =$ 2000 - 2500 kg/m^3

c) $\rho =$ 1800 - 2200 kg/m^3

d)$\rho =$ 500 - 1800 kg/m^3

3. What aggregates are used to make heavy (normal) concrete?

a)On dense aggregate (granite, marble, gravel, etc.).

b)On porous coarse aggregate (vermiculite, expanded clay, aglopyrite, etc.).

c)On especially heavy aggregates (magnesite, barite, steel scraps, etc.).

d)On pumice, volcanic tuffs, etc.

4. What concretes are there according to the nature of the structure?

a)Concretes with a dense (cohesive) structure in which the space between the aggregate grains is completely occupied by the hardened binder.

b)Coarse-porous concrete (sandless or low-sand concrete) in which a significant portion of the intergranular void volume is left unoccupied by fine aggregate and hardened binder.

c)Porous concrete in which the space between the aggregate grains is occupied by a binder porous with foam or gas-forming additives.

d)All of the above answers are correct.

5. Under what circumstances is concrete delamination (reduction in concrete density) observed?

a)When cement consumption increases.

b)Insufficient cement content in concrete.

c)When shrinkage deformations develop.

d)When the crack resistance of concrete is reduced.

6. Under what circumstances does the activity of cement decrease?

a)When mixing the concrete mixture vigorously.

b)When cement is mixed with additives (cement hardening gas pedals).

c)When storing it in warehouses.

d)All answers are correct.

7. What property characterizes the internal cohesion of a concrete mixture, its ability to be molded, acquiring a given shape without breaks and delamination?

a)Plasticity of the concrete mix.

b)Concrete mix mobility.

c)Concrete Strength.

d)Frost resistance of concrete.

8. What properties of a concrete mix determine the mobility of the concrete mix?

a)The ability of a concrete mix to spread due to its own weight and the cohesiveness of the concrete mix.

b)The property characterizes the internal cohesion of the concrete mixture, its ability to be molded into a given shape without breaking or delamination.

c)The ability of concrete to keep water out under pressure.

d)The property of concrete to retain when exposed to high temperatures for short periods of time.

9. Which property of concrete characterizes its frost resistance?

a)The ability of concrete to keep water out under pressure.

b)The ability of water-saturated concrete to retain strength and not collapse when alternately frozen and thawed.

c)The property of concrete to retain when exposed to high temperatures for short periods of time.

d)The ability of a concrete mixture to spread due to its own weight and the cohesiveness of the concrete mixture.

10. What is meant by water-cement ratio?

a)The ratio of water weight to cement weight in a freshly made concrete mix, only the free water, not the water absorbed by the aggregate, is taken into account. During curing, depending on the quality and curing time, cement only absorbs 15-25% of water from the mass of cement.

b)To give the concrete mixture plasticity in the concrete add much more water (40-70% of the weight of cement, B/C = 0.4-0.7), because at B/C = 0.2 concrete mixture is almost dry, and it can not be qualitatively mixed and placcd.

c)The strength of concrete increases as the water-cement ratio decreases.

d)All answers are correct.

11. What is the guaranteed strength of concrete in MPa with a confidence level of 0.95?

a) B

b)M

c)B

d)W

12. What does the standardized value of the average strength of concrete in kgf/cm(2) (MPa) indicate?

a) B

b)M

c) Б

d)W

13. Which property of concrete best resists compression?

a)Mobility.

b)Frost resistance.

c)Durability.

d)Waterproof.

14. How can the normal curing condition of concrete in winter be ensured?

a)Application of high-strength and fast-setting cements.

b) Reduce water-cement ratio and intensive compaction of the concrete mixture

c) Introduce curing gas pedals (calcium chloride, etc.) into the concrete mix.

d)All answers are correct.

15. What is the name of the concrete used in hydraulic structures for concreting thin-walled densely reinforced structures with complex configurations?

a)Cast Concrete.

b)Fine Concrete.

c)Concretes for radiation shielding.

d)Decorative Concretes.

16. What is the name of the concrete used to finish structural strips of roadways, etc.?

a)Heavy Concrete.

b)Lightweight concrete.

c)Decorative Concrete.

d)Road Concrete.

17. Under what conditions does concrete cure?

a)At natural hardening, hardening at 1=15-20°C and atmospheric pressure.

b)Concretes subjected to heat treatment (70-90°C) at atmospheric pressure to accelerate curing.

c)Concretes curing in autoclaves at 1=175-200°C and vapor pressure 0.9-1.6MPa.

d)All answers are correct.

18. What is the name of the concrete used to make load-bearing and enclosing precast

concrete and reinforced concrete structures, used instead of bricks and heavy concrete?

a)Lightweight Concretes.

b)Lightweight Concretes.

c)Particularly lightweight concretes.

d)Particularly Heavy Concretes.

19. According to what lightweight concrete is divided into expanded clay concrete, agloporite concrete, slag concrete, pumice concrete, etc.?

a)Depending on the type of coarse aggregate used.

b)Depending on the type of fine aggregate used.

c)Depending on the type of binder used.

d)Depending on the type of additives used.

20. Which lightweight concretes with average density are structurally - thermally insulating lightweight concretes? $\rho = 500 - 1800\ kg/m^3$

a)$\rho = 500\ kg/m^3$, used for the manufacture of thermal insulation boards and other products.

b)$\rho = 500\text{-}1400\ kg/m^3$, used in load-bearing and self-supporting enclosing structures (walls and floors).

c)$\rho = 1400 - 1800\ kg/m^3$ used in load-bearing structures.

d)$\rho = 1800 - 2200\ kg/m^3$ used for walls, slabs and coverings.

Correct answers

1 - c	5 - b	9 - b	13 - c	17 - d
2 - a	6 - c	10 - b	14 - d	18 - a
3 - a	7 - a	11 - a	15 - a	19 - a
4 - d	8 - a	12 - b	16 - c	20- b

LITERATURE

1. Bazhenov Y.M. Technology of concrete. M. Higher School. 2003г. 500с.

2. Vorobyev V.A., Komar A.G. "Construction materials". Publishing house of literature on construction. M. 1971, pp. 496.

3. Gorchakov G.I., Bazhenov Y.M. Building materials. M. Stroyizdat. 1986г. 688с.

4. Gorchakov G.I., Bazhenov. YU.M. "Construction materials". Stroyizdat. M., 1986. Page 687

5. Komar A.G. "Building materials and products". Higher School. M.1988. pp. 527.

6. Korchagina O.A. Designing of composition of heavy, light and silicate concrete. Tambov. Publishing house of GOU VPO TSTU. 2010г.

7. Osnovin V.N., Shulyakov L.V., Dubyago D.S. Reference book on building materials and products. Edition of the fifth. "Phoenix" 2009g. 448с.

8. Khiregovich M.I., Gorchakov G.I. and others. "Construction materials". Stroyizdat. M. 1970. Pp. 368.

9. podomostroim.ru Winter concreting.

10. gardenweb.ru>klassifikatsiya-betonov Classification of concretes.

MIX
Papier aus verantwortungsvollen Quellen
Paper from responsible sources
FSC® C105338

FSC
www.fsc.org

Printed by Books on Demand GmbH, Norderstedt / Germany